THE BLUE HOUR

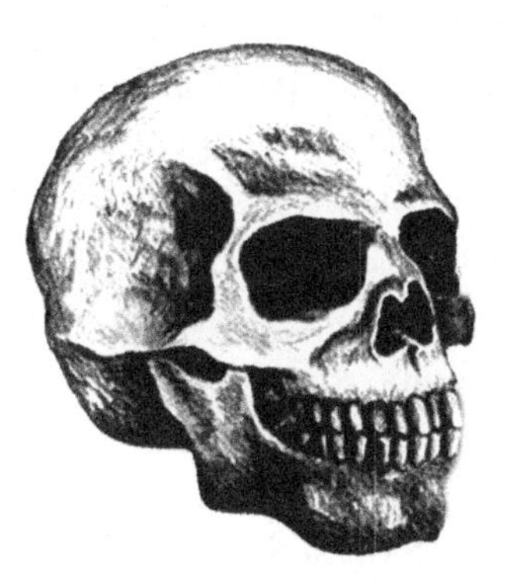

James Lilley

UNCLE B. PUBLICATIONS
Indianapolis, Indiana

The Blue Hour

First Printing, November 2021

Cover Design by Tia Ja'nae.

ISBN: 978-1-957034-01-0

Dedicated to the memory of
Amjed Haddad
(1986-2019)

For my wife, daughters and son who put up with all my stuff.

CONTENTS

The Family Man

He came home from the murder
spending the evening on the sofa
with his children
he laughed with them,
at family feud
they didn't notice inside
he was filled
with killings and lists
All that he'd done
A void of darkness
he kissed his daughter and wife
good night and left again
on orders
just another body
another bill paid
the family man.

Thoughts

Thoughts, raven-wing like, fluttering swarm at night,
claws me into depths of black.
An abandoned prison, with cells empty,
full of changing shadows,
outreaching arms of dread,
Come they call.
Ever scratching,
Thoughts of dark swallowing me whole
wondering if the ceiling beam
will hold my weight.

Dog Walks

I walk my dog early
to avoid people
to be on my own
Taking in nature, the lane by
the river, which is alive and vibrant,
Curious horses approach from a nearby field, questioning,
My cava chon cowers behind my legs.

I walk my dog early,
to avoid breakfast arguments
to think,
the lane meanders right, sharp left until,
a man-made scar,
reaching a high tide flooded river,
surface calm, unmoving, sun shining
off the surface creating
a million sparkling diamonds,
in flight a graceful heron.
Almost a dancer,
gliding along shimmering expanse,
darts its beak, it hunts, into the blue
retrieving a fish, questioning,
much to annoyance of men in tents.
Filling my lungs, closing my eyes,
with clear crisp air.
Forgetting.

I walk my dog early,
for peace
for time,
taking a longer way back,
A pair of glowing yellow eyes
watching from under bush,
Sniggering fox
knowing.

Wind whispers through trees,
I walk my dog early,
they get longer
each time
Until I am lost.

Docks

I can't tell you,
how beautiful a summer evening it was
early July,
dazzling sun peeking
when they pulled her body from the docks.
Bloated pale and dripping wet,
air filled with smells of rotting flesh and seaweed.
A small crowd gathered
Choked
The fish had eaten her eyes
as they lay you on the concrete covering
you with a sheet.

Flowers

Withered curling brown petals
fall from bouquet of dead flowers
floating to rest
beside her where she was pulled from the stinking water.

Tossed aside and forgotten
to be found in repulsion
like the flowers
saccharine decomposing scent drifting
a shrine of death.

From Danygraig to Qibla

From high up in Danygraig
the morning, we bid farewell,
looking over the bay
greys swell and roll.
Bursting sprinkling the hill in a light drizzle
they opened the box.
You were shrouded, in unblemished, white cloth
in contrast to the colours of green trees, brown dirt, black suits,
a crowd a merge of cultures,
united in remembering.
Sun seeps through,
Illuminating the grief,
Oh how brief,
weeps to God, Duw and Allah
Yet I whisper to the breeze.
By hand we cover you gently, all that is left is a mound.
Rain covered tears, mud covered hand
only a moment, not long gone.
Where softly turned east, and laid you Qibla in the ground.

Veil

I feel it clinging to me
the veil of death
everywhere.
Unshakeable a booming ticking of the clock
Oh how fragile
Surviving under the veil.

Caine

My new friend
feels like forever
time stretches when we are together.
Pain subsides, to a gentle
throb.
Pulse beneath the surface that old familiar twitch
quick as I burn, we feel
elevated
that rush.
We met in the doctor's surgery,
last time I sought help.

Cycle

Skull white powder, little plastic bag,
safe in the cycle, insecure in society,
forever the last time,
dawn breaks, darkness retreats.

Habit

Ceiling fan whirred,
unrelenting suffocation June heat,
snow white duster table tops,
goose bumped pale flesh
shivering cold sweat.
Gasping unending demand,
chemical pain release
free from the ache,
Trapped in the habit.

The Snap

Curios yellow eyes watched,
in the twilight
from corner concealed
in shadow
tail flicking
as woman paced
vinyl kitchen floor
she talked but only
to herself
bowl of decaying fruit
saccharine odour filled the air
neither minded
it masked the smell of man
sat slumped at dinner table
face black and bloated
tongue lolling covered white
dead milky eyes wondering when
the snap occurred
she began dicing veg
noticing not kitchen blade
sliced finger tip
off
cackling in the night
Cat purred wondering when
the snap occurred

Decaying Streets

Under slither of moon, I walk on empty decaying streets.
Shattered windows of abandoned stores,
like empty eyes boring into me.
I try to find a place to stop
with my only friend
warming my pocket
he is purest white
powdered bliss on these decaying streets
of a dying town,
leaves me gasping.

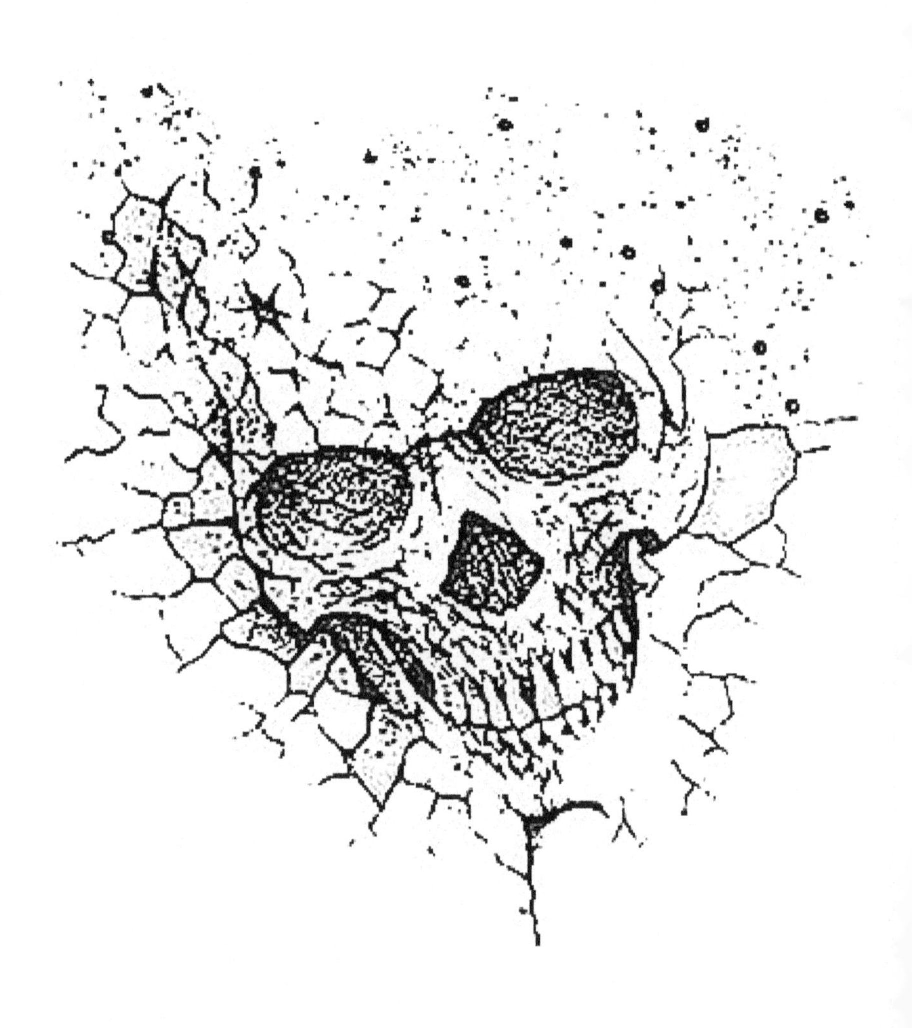

Different Bells

I jingle, the empty bottle of bells,
swerving all the way,
Oh what fun it is to be addict,
I always have to act the prick.

Safe

Lying by my side,
I feel safe,
Here, with you.

A storm incensed outdoors, our home a ship.
Weather battered haven, a refuge of love built,
free from guilt.

Lying by my side,
I feel safe, here with you.

Awake

Motorcycle roar rips me
from warmth of dreams
like cold water splashed on my face,
Eyes heavy, pulling me back to slumber

What was that?

Questioning neurones fire off
refusing the pull back under
I turn, toss, trying to hide
shake voices off
a watermark on whitewashed walls
catches my eye
in gloom, resembling
twisted screaming mouth.

Choir of voices begin to babble
shout, echoing
so deafening in the still darkness
of my bedroom.
Loved one snoozing sweetly.

Where were they going?

2.30am blinks from bedside clock
slithering from under sheets
creeping downstairs
each tip toe resonates

Shhh!

Voice beckon, ravenous
laptop clicks open
cigarette ignited burning orange ember
illuminates face, a ghastly mask in

dead screen.
Windows bong thunders and shakes
house
I freeze
voices do not cease.
I cannot write
creative choked by motorcycle roar
voices awakened,
moment gone.

Neon Wash

Sitting near dirty window
Washed in a grotesque
unnatural pink light
pulsing, almost alive
from neon sign.
O'Malleys.
Flickering no one likes to sit in its glare
buzzing so loud, drills into you
piercing skull
shaking teeth.
I have as long as I need
Barman doesn't mind
he locks up when I leave.
Bourbons burn keeps me warm
comfort blanket in the
Neon Wash.

Morning Routine

Ringing splits the air, my head in two
pulling from the clinging warmth of bed.
Trudging over to cracked reflection fluorescent flickering tubes
sting bloodshot eyes.
Too ashamed to look at cracked reflection
watching back.
Down to get coffee
caffeine chasing liquor from veins.
Air hangs heavy with stale whiskey
mound of butts over spilling ashtray
traces of powder lining work top
run a finger
between clenched teeth.
Head out the door
work begins at four.

Interview

Long sleeved shirt, to hide my arms,
Those fucking scars, from when I was sixteen,
Angry kid, nowhere to vent
I turn up early, to make a good impression.

Consumption

Ignorance is bliss
once it takes hold
we become one
a rapid descent
a need so great
it consumes me.

Crawl

You smelled beautiful the day
you made me crawl away
I watched from down in the dirt,
a worm,
as you left
an open wound ripped in my heart.
This pain is just the fucking start.

Bleed For This

Bright red drips from above my eye
pooling on sky blue canvas as I kneel
almost a prayer.
Get up.

Final examination takes place
under burning naked lights
all those weeks
hard work forgotten
They want blood and you oblige
dancing to a beat
Bare fist cracks like a whip
Crooked teeth split lip swollen knuckles
beautiful violence an art form
where to destroy is to create
you cannot quit that is the ultimate shame

You rise. Inhale.
Pushing down nerves, pushing down fear
one last hurrah like the light brigade
but there will be no medals
or commendations.

Unforgiving eyes watch on
you sweat for this
you cry for this
you bleed for this.

Drain

Vital red pulls and breaks
in swirl of rusted drain
mouth yawn
gaggling in the trickle
.

Valium doesn't work anymore
I don't even feel numb
pain bites
adding in the pill bottle
shake, rattle and roll.
Twenty should be enough.

Tremble

Trembling, under sheets I reach across
the vacant space
seeking the love and comfort
we once held dear.
Now dispersed
crumbled like a fine white powder
search across the expanse of our bed
that was only inches but felt
more void like
cold.
I cannot find her.
There's just a note instead

Drift

So I drift
ignoring phone chimes
unpaid bills
reaching across for comfort
but I find only space and cold
where you used to lay.

So I drift
using sick days
letters mounting
doors knocking
curtains always closed
hiding from day
never seeing night.

So I drift
No dog to walk
I float from room to room
quiet is deafening
So I drift.

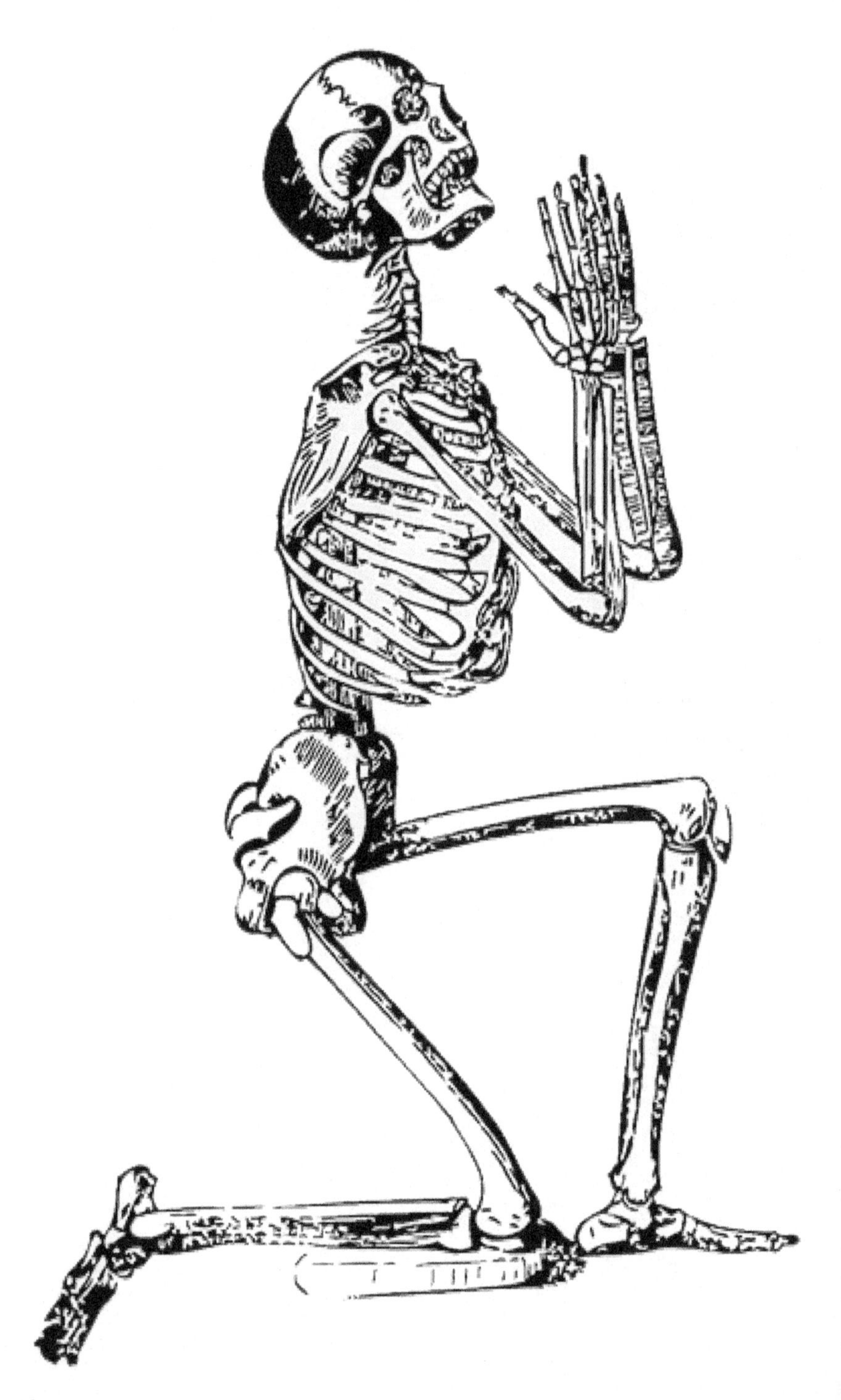

Angel

Praying forgiveness,
she nestled into the crook of my elbow
I noticed pinprick scars
in the crook of her elbow.
She kneels but not to pray
You having a good time baby?
Passing rolled up twenty
We got time
Oh there's plenty
Crushing pills beneath
room service menu
Angel, they call her
wanting salvation
some warmth
no God in room 201.

Reconnecting

I sought help during lockdown
zoom sessions only
waiting to connect, I felt the disconnect
A stranger on a screen
Asking about my past.
How many secrets can a stranger keep?
Reconnecting. Please wait.
Deliberately dishonest discussions
She asks, I reply
calculated admissions
No one had noticed I wasn't okay
'Open up'
'Connect'
replied the shape on the screen
Reconnecting. Please wait.
Anyone close you can talk to?
Strange world restrictions
She waits for me to continue
(or is she buffering?)
Reconnecting. Please wait.
Not the help I wanted.
For 40 an hour.

Permanent Way

We walked on disused tracks, hopeful.
Sky a million shades of pink
Low winter sun sinking,
draining days warmth with it
aside metal rails
Ground littered with shoes, cans, wrappers
ants, beetles crawling feverishly amongst
belongings stuff in small pack.
Following the permanent way
Stepping over sleepers
creeping between discarded needles
mood reflective like the sun
sparkling off them
because of what came before
behind us.
Passing rusted warped town marker
Empty factories watching with haunted cracked windows.
Calling.
As we passed from one life
to the next.

Emerge

From a dream
thousand regrets
blanket of comfort
A pocket companion.
Thrown to the wind
breathing is easy
living is hard
so eager to melt
Promises
to keep from the
dark.
I emerge.

13

Contender

Tonight's not your night kid
Resonated in my head
as I made the walk
through crowd
faceless merciless horde
they wanted a show
promoter wanted a sure thing
hitting sky blue canvas
blood staining
corner urging
stay down
This ain't your night
Didn't even try
took the money
crying into my coach's arms
I could have been a contender.

Final Call

Twelve months it took me to visit,
Life sometimes gets in the way,
Standing in freezing December rain
I cried and said my goodbye
She grasped my hand the warmth
a burning love
a forgiveness
the rain washed us clean.

The Blue Hour

Just before sunrise, in the blue hour,
where the sky is deep blue, suffused with cerulean light
I head for the shore.
Meandering down through winding roads, shadows stretch long, yet to retreat,
with the moons ghost burning bright hanging low.
Crossing Dylan's park its deathly silent, no bird song or bush rustle.
Bare tree branches beckon, woods gently whisper, as I descend the cobbled hill, beside haunting Tudor houses with dead windows
looming large on either side of street.
Sneaking quietly to where the sky and sea meet, the wide sandy bay meets the dimness of an unbroken dawn.
Crashing sounds of waves, salty breeze,
accompany Abertawe strolls in the blue hour.
Where I walk to remember.

Grin

I left the den
forgetting shoes
probably minus two
toes were numb despite
fluffy Christmas Socks.

Stopping at 24 hour liquor store
light from window spilling onto curb
pockets empty
I asked the homeless guy
sitting outside
if he had any spare change
he grinned a toothless smile
I've only got my amex.
He cackled.

View From The Hill

Vivid views from Pantycelyn steps
so good it should be on a postcard
combined with orange glow
suffocating smoke
from burning car wrecks.

Early nineties
population less that eight thousand
a tiny council estate became
the car crime capital of Europe.

High speed chases
through sleepy streets
dumping brand new motors
just for a laugh
only twocking in Abertawe

Police chief called it the *Wild West*
kids wouldn't go to school
but could boost and drive
by the time they were twelve.

Old lady won a mini in the pools
they found it two days later
at the bottom of Cockett Park
twisted blackened metal
its only twocking in Abertawe.

Therapy in Different Form

I beat with bloody fist
leaving red smudges and dents
I scream with hoarse voice
vile words and obscenities
I sob until no tears come
head rested on
I don't speak for days
silence deafening
my bedroom wall bares it all
with no judgement.

Nothing Really Bothers Me

I'm better than just ok
things are all just swell
when I take my
Flouextine caps
twice daily

Sometimes

Sometime the car wouldn't start
to save embarrassment I'd just
look down
at brown water
pooled in the well
below my feet
in the back there was a hole
where you could see through
to the floor and
watch the road passing by.

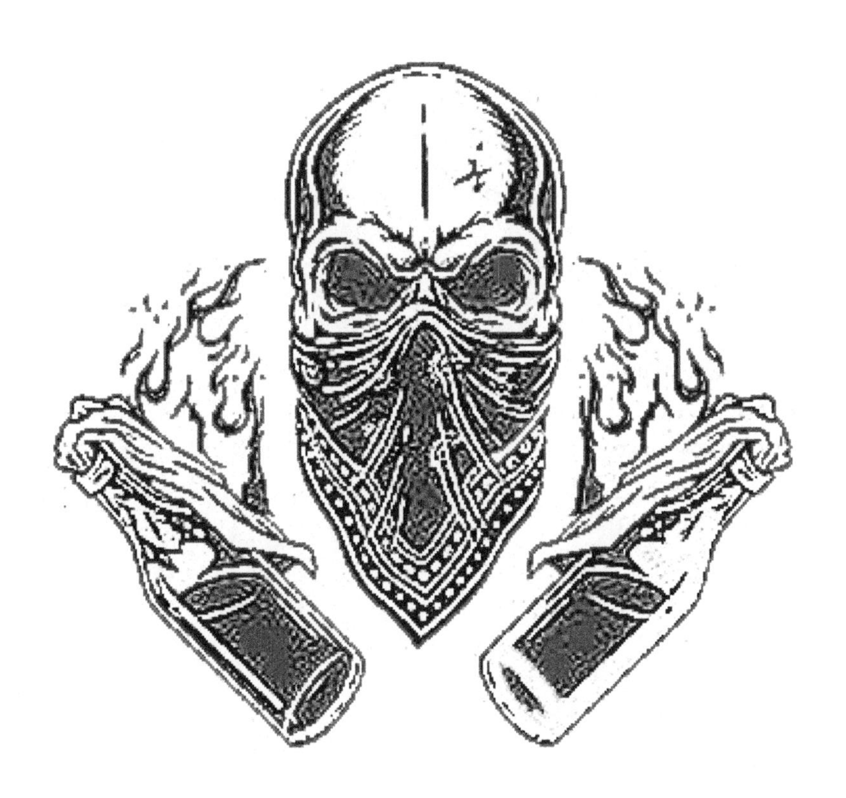

Stash House

A pattering outside
Sounds like heavy rain on the windows
Maybe its fireworks
but its March 3rd
Cloud of blue smoke
Chevrolet speeds off
They were meant to hit a stash house,
Stench of gunpowder
singes nostril hair,
Family of four got caught instead
house full of holes
When they pulled the bodies out
People collapsed in the street
Screaming to the Gods
They'd opened up with a mac 10
Caught a guy
he proclaimed sorry
into news camera
Not sure what to make of it all.

Acts of Violence

I hated high school
Fake Adidas poppers,
wrong postcode
Slipknot hoodies
walking the long way home
avoiding kids from the estate
joint butts
and mitching
in the woods
with the goths.

Nu metal records
and half cuts of vodka
in the café on high street
just to get through the week
mouthy kid from the hill
I fucking hated high school.

Hardest Words

Making a mistake is easy
admitting to it isn't
so here I am
telling you I was wrong
I want to start again.

Autumn Kiss

Watching from park bench
when autumn died
she did so in a fire of a thousand pinks.
Painting the sunset sky in a palette of shades
colours I have no names for
of unequalled beauty
warmth reflection of sinking sun.
Dusk dusted trees dance gently
yellowing leaves curl away in sadness
the last of bright nights
So shadows grow long and frost
will bite and gnaw.
We sigh together for our
departing lover, leaving with a kiss
My aching heart.

Sleeping Alone

I read somewhere
that humans are meant to
sleep alone
figures suggest
you are likely to have a more
restful slumber
when you are alone.

This does not explain why
I keep waking
wondering
where
you
are.

The Girl With The Bright Red Hair

After last orders,
and the lights came on
people spilled from
bars onto the cobble street.

I spotted a girl
with bright red hair
leaning against glass window
lit fag in hand
smoke dancing around her face.

I asked if she
would like to party
she politely declined
fuck you then,
Was my ungentlemanly reply.

A week later she found me
inbox one new message
she called me rude and
the girl with bright red hair
five years later
whispered I do.

Note on a Bridge

Winter in a t-shirt
bare arms patterned in
goose bumps
shivering I climb rail
cars rushing by underneath
headlights dazzling
cold wind whipping
pulling at me
I notice paper
flapping
curiously unfolding
Never too late to turn back
and a phone number
I went home
but never called.

Forget More Please, So I Can Pretend

Sometimes you forget
That you hate me
Resting your feet in my lap
Or kissing me as I leave
For work
Laughing at my shit jokes
Showing all your teeth
Sometimes you forget
And I can pretend
We were just like
Before.

Isolation

In a house full of people
being lonely is different this year
Not going outside or anywhere for that matter
anxiety is different this year
Over a hundred thousand deaths
depression is different this year
eating to the pass the time
body image is different this year
Everyone is wearing mask and I can't read faces
Being nervous is different this year.
Creativity stifled and choked
Writing poetry is different this year.

Salesman

I stopped selling
and just use now instead
makes it easier to keep track
and get lost
without worrying about numbers
I was never any good at maths anyway.

Lonely Room

No one came to the changing room
when I was defeated
they didn't want to
see my swollen face or shattered ego
to ashamed to show them
I was crying while
they stitched my eye.

Blueberries and Rain

We snuck into roofless church
inside devastated by fire
few years back
she took me by the hand
as the rain came down
leading me between
remaining pews
whisper scared
as if God cared
she kissed me by the alter
tasting of blueberries and tobacco
passing me the cheap side
softly asking me
not to leave
falling asleep
under a starless sky.

Bandages

Having hands wrapped for the hundredth time
probably more.
face littered with scars
each one a memory
most a lesson
no matter how sweet the victory,
A wise man once told me
the brain is weaker
after you reach thirty-four
but I carry on regardless
the pain my favourite companion
nothing comes close
you don't lose 'til you quit
but something is lost
every time.

Amjed

Seems so long
that you have
been gone
but only yesterday
you left my house
getting fucked up with the boys
checking outside for cars
that weren't there
all dressed up
to stand in my kitchen
I check whatsapp
Last online
23/10/19
I know you're somewhere.

All The Trivial Things

We see different counsellors
but we don't talk about
what we talk about
at dinner
we push peas around the
plate
and comment on
the steak
we don't talk about
what we talk about
making awkward conversation
about Sue at work
our neighbours car
next years holiday
we hide from each other
behind all the trivial things.

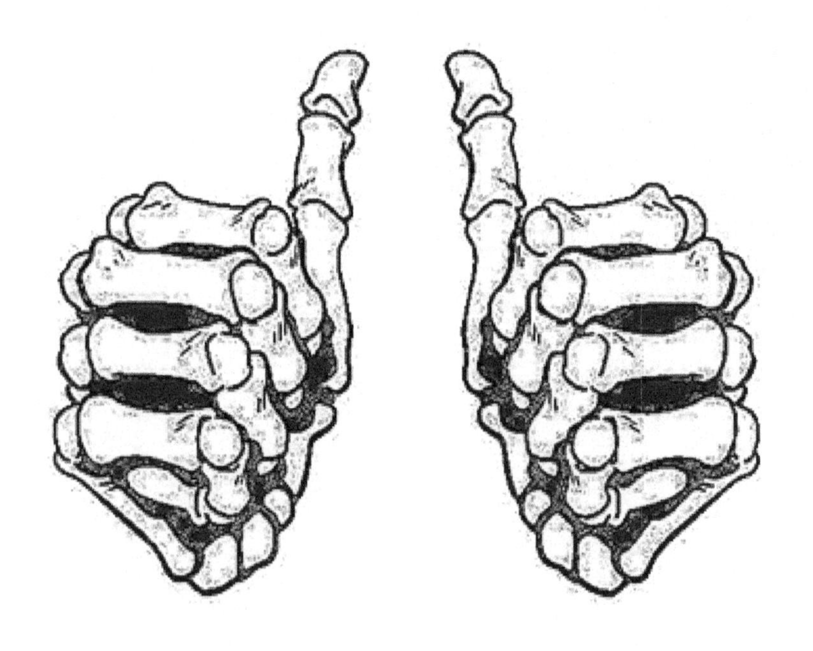

Blanketing *(With Amy-Jean Muller)*

And the weight of it
In its brilliance of flawless white
All pure
Everything
Clean
Wraps me in the Bedouin of blanketing
This snow
This snow
But
freedom knows
The pull crush and claw,
Heart pressed to the floor
Fear until the thaw….
Melts the charade
Exposing the rot
Lest we
Forget….
And decay

Minotaur *(With Wayne Jermin)*

Trapped in the labyrinth of my mind
Elaborate, confusing maze
A dead end at every turn, almost,
Unanswered questions
Scratching whispering walls
Mistakes made
Decisions questioned,
Stuck searching for the centre
For the answers
for acceptance.
Blinder by blood
shaped by darkness
no monsters to seek
or defeat
shadows with voices
tempting dark fate
fear turns to aggression
I take it out on myself
No short cuts
no escape
locked in with I,

Sorrow *(With B F Jones)*

My faith left when the streets emptied
Roller-coasters running with no riders
Town full of ghosts
Something no longer there
Not known by name
Innumerable dread.

My faith left
When I stumbled upon discarded
Party balloons and love corals
Remnants of a life that no longer is
Swept away by plastic waves
Of toxic sludge.

THE BLUE HOUR

Acknowledgements

I would like to extend a huge thank you and acknowledge the following publications where some of these poems were originally published, sometimes with slight changes, I am forever grateful.

Versification
Black Bough Poetry
Fevers of the Mind Poetry
Close to the Bone
Punk Noir Magazine
The Five- Two
Splintered Disorder Press
Dead Fern Press
Skyward Journal
Alien Buddha Press
ExPat Lit

There are a few people I would like to extend a special thank you to Stephen J. Golds who believed in my work and took a chance. C. Cimmone and the Versification team who have supported and helped me on this journey. Amy-Jean Muller and Matthew C. Smith. Without the encouragement, guidance, inspiration and general chat from the people listed I probably wouldn't of made it this far, admittedly I probably wouldn't have submitted my first poem.

Sion , Jamie , Max , Wayne, Barb, Scott and everyone else I speak to regularly I thank you for letting me share some of my work with you.

Tisa and Alec and the Uncle B team I am forever grateful.

Barb, Scott and the rest of the punk posse for having my back.

Of course my Wife, Stacey and children Bella, Ruby and Tommy. You don't know it but you guys are my inspiration.

Amjed I miss you brother. Until we meet again these are for you.

Praise for The Blue Hour

It would be too simplistic to call James Lilley's debut poetry collection hard-hitting, because it's so much more than that. Tackling a range of themes from modern-day masculinity, relationships - as a father, a lover, a fighter and a friend - and the internal fight against depression and addiction, Lilley's words pack an emotional gut-punch. One that will stay with you long into the Blue Hour itself.

--- J.P Seabright, author and assistant editor of Full House Literary Magazine.

James Lilley writes with brutal honesty and stunning simplicity about lives caught between day and night. With The Blue Hour, he has emerged as one of our most arresting new poets.

--- Max Thrax, author of Gods Is A Killer

James Lilley's debut collection is a true accomplishment from the very first page. From within Lilley's deeply considered contemplations, Blue Hour becomes steeped in meaning as much as the title itself. A period where the shades of dawn form a junction with the conclusion of twilight, Blue Hour illustrates how even the most beautiful can cut the heart with darkness and melancholy. Lilley has championed a truly heroic and honest account of the bleakness we face as humans, the expectations of masculinity, the folly of our humanness, and gently offers a softness that shows that even the darkest of nights can be met with the possibility of a new day.

--- Amy-Jean Muller, Artist and Author of Baptism By Fire

In this collection of short and punchy poems, Lilley mixes the beauty of Welsh scenery and the comfort of a bedroom at dawn with the brutality of a world full of regret, loss, crime and addiction. James Lilley's vision of the world is at the same time gaunt and colorful, soft and harsh; he finds beauty in ugliness and ugliness in beauty and lays it all on a mesmerizing canvas: rips and tears and blood drops on a delicate pastel landscape.

--- B F Jones, author of The Only Sounds Left and Artifice

A very powerful and honest collect of Punk poetry at its finest. Lilley speaks from the heart and writes off the cuff brining his personal experiences to life straight off the page.

A gritty mixture of crime, addiction, mental health and love, The Blue Hour captivates from the very first line.

Lilley has the ability to capture heart-felt moments, personal tragedy and survival in such a devastating way. It will certainly get you in the gut as well as the heart.

--- Wayne Jermin, author of Hang The Sad Pictures

Indianapolis, Indiana

Made in the USA
Las Vegas, NV
16 December 2021